GW01401105

OFFB[

by
JOHN C. CHADWICK

Cover Photography by BOB CROXFORD
Atmosphere Picture Library 0326 240180

ISBN No. 0 907683 38 X

Published by:-
Nigel J. Clarke Publications,
Unit 2,
Russell House,
Lyme Regis,
Dorset.

CONTENTS

The help given by the staff of Wilton Public Library is gratefully acknowledged.

INTRODUCTION

You may think it presumptuous to add even another millimetre to the mountain already written about Bath. But there seems to be room for something which appeals to lovers of the offbeat. This little book attempts to meet that need.

Following a visit to the city's centre, five walkabouts describe the curiosities of the past — people, features and events — to be found on the way. Each walk takes around 1½ to 2 hours (excluding interiors) and can of course be joined at any point.

Sauntering along the streets, terraces and crescents of Bath, the chief attraction is the unspoilt splendour of its classical stone buildings. Surrounding woods and the River Avon add to the pleasure.

ORIGINS

The Leper Swineherd

What is now one of Europe's most beautiful cities got off to a very strange start around 800 BC. According to the legend, in a remote part of Somerset a swineherd suffering from leprosy was tending his pigs, which also became infected. They used to wallow in some hot springs by a river bank and one day he noticed that they came out cured. So he did the same and cured himself too.

This was no ordinary swineherd but a prince named Bladud, son of the British king Lud Hudibras, who had banished him from court on account of his disease. Restored to favour, Bladud spent some years in Greece studying magic, philosophy and mathematics. Home again and on the throne, he developed his healing springs at Bath (Kaerbadus) where he built a palace and a city round it. He is supposed to have sired King Lear, before crashing to his death in an attempt to fly with home-made wings.

Musical Churchyard

Today Bath's focal point is the vicinity of Abbey Churchyard, which links the Roman Baths, the Abbey itself and the Pump Room. Last year it attracted 873, 414 visitors (second to the Tower of London in the National League). Entertainers enliven the scene — an early Grecian plays his pipes of Pan, a Georgian dandy his recorder, fiddlers scrape, fluters tootle and a medieval jester jokes. Before any exploration begins, a visit is recommended to the three principal features here, because they continue the city's background from Bladud onwards.

THE ROMAN BATHS

Gossip and Ritual

In the barbarous colony of Britain, with its filthy weather, the ruling Romans missed their beloved public baths. There they not only kept fit but also exchanged the latest titbits of gossip. ("Have you heard about Mark Antony going off with that dreadful Cleopatra?") So they were quick to expand Bladud's hot springs.

The Romans would have been drawn to the main spring by an adjacent Celtic shrine dedicated to the local deity Sulis. They joined her to their own goddess Minerva, for whom they built a temple. The Sacred Spring was contained within a reservoir and used to supply a large bathing complex close to the temple. This turned Bath (now Aquae Sulis) into a spa which thrived between the first and fourth centuries AD. Ptolemy, a chronicler of those times, called it one of the Wonders of the World.

Moles at Work

Entering the Roman Baths from Abbey Churchyard, you can inspect the remains of their buildings about 10 to 20 feet below street level. These were first discovered in 1755 and excavated late last century by a rather careless City Architect, Major Charles Davis, who destroyed a lot of valuable fragments. Recent excavations have revealed further objects which are on view in the fascinating underground museum.

Curious Curses

The Sacred Spring not only provided hot water but was also the place for getting in touch with the goddess Sulis-Minerva. Votive offerings were thrown in and more than 12,000 have been found, as well as gem stones, metal jugs and cups. Other offerings took the form of curses scratched on pewter sheets and intended to bring vengeance on the wrongdoer.

About ninety of these curiosities were recovered. Here is one displayed example, written backwards to baffle everyone but the goddess:

"May he who carried off Vilbia from me become as liquid as the water, may she who so obscenely devoured her become dumb, whether Velvinna, Exsupereus, Severinus, Augustalia, Comitianus, Catusminianus, Germanilla or Jovina."

Another curse promised a cloak to the goddess if she caused the death of Maximus, who had stolen it.

Romans Relax

The Great Bath was fed direct from the Spring and the drainage system, which still operates today, is said to be "the oldest functioning sewer in Britain." But the Roman emperors' statues on top of the wall are late-Victorian. Here was the heart of the whole covered bathing complex, which eventually included cold plunges, saunas, Turkish baths, exercise courts and undressing rooms. After exercise, the bathers would graduate from the tepid to the sweating room. Then, oiled, scraped and massaged, they finished up with a quick cold plunge.

It was all very lively and sociable with board games and business transactions thrown in. Slaves and servants milled about among the jugglers, manicurists and gamblers. The carvings on the tombs and slabs you see show that the bath-users came from all over Europe. There was Julius Vitalis, a Belgic tribesman of the 20th Legion, Tancinus, a cavalryman from Spain, Priscius, a Gaulish stonemason and Peregrinus from Trier on the German border.

The Gorgon's Sex-change

In 1727 a workman engaged on sewage improvements made a startling discovery. It was the life-size gilded bromze head of the goddess Minerva, though without her customary helmet. Now one of the highlights of the underground tour, this serene and dignified face somehow symbolises the graciousness of Georgian Bath.

Minerva's statue would have adorned the Roman temple which adjoined the baths. Steps led up to four large columns supporting a pediment. Its dominating feature has survived — a frightening head of the Gorgon Medusa. She was the mythological creature who had snakes for hair and whose gaze turned men to stone. But in this vivid Celtic-style carving it is a man who is portrayed, with a billowing beard and bulging eyes. The reason for the change is obscure but Minerva used to carry a shield bearing a Gorgon's head on it.

Sacrificial Relics

Outside the temple stood the sacrificial altar, decorated with carved deities on its four corners. The parts on show feature Jupiter, Hercules and Bacchus. Sheep, pigs and cattle were sacrificed, their livers being used to foretell the future.

It seems strange that these remarkable remains do not include some traces of a theatre, usually an essential part of Roman life: one day perhaps something will be found.

THE ABBEY
The Medical Bishop

After the collapse of the Roman Empire, the Saxons put up an abbey at what they called Akemanceaster or later Bathanceaster. Replacing a small Celtic church and sited to the east of the present Abbey, Edgar the first King of All England was crowned there in AD 973.

When the haughty Norman Bishop of Bath, John de Villula, found this abbey in ruins, he superseded it with a vast cathedral. He was also a physician and revived the hot springs set-up, which was controlled by the Church.

Desecration

Four hundred years later in 1499, this building was in turn "ruined to its foundations" thanks to the neglect of its worldly priors. So the new Bishop, Oliver King, started constructing the present Abbey. But with interruptions like the Dissolution of the Monasteries, when the place was stripped of its bells, lead, glass, wood and iron, the work did not finish until the 17th century. It was no larger than the nave of its predecessor.

A Stone Portrait Gallery

The exterior is imposing but does not overwhelm you. It blends well with its surroundings and there is no need for the usual spacious close. The west front dominates Abbey Churchyard. The impression is of a huge window, rich pinnacles and elegant turrets — all clean vertical lines except for the angles of the flying buttresses.

Above the window is a statue of Our Lord, with the Heavenly Host at his feet and at the bottom a

Victorian one of King Henry VII: the twelve apostles appear beside it. The main door has the Montague arms profusely carved in oak and is guarded by St. Paul and St. Peter, who seems to have lost his neck. The spandrels show emblems of the Passion.

The Bishop's Rebus

The story goes that before Bishop King began to build the Abbey he had a curious dream. In it he saw a ladder to heaven with angels mounting and descending. Then he heard a voice saying: "Let an Olive establish the Crown and a King restore the Church." This he took to be a celestial go-ahead for the project.

A version of the dream is portrayed in the two ladders with angels, flanking the great west window. Why one of the angels is coming down head first is not clear — perhaps a fall from grace. The Bishop's rebus (or punning logo) also appears at the foot of each ladder — an olive tree rising up from a crown surmounted by a mitre.

"The Lantern of the West"

Inside, the Abbey is bathed in light from its fifty-two windows. No wonder it is called "The Lantern of the West." Up above the aisles, chancel and nave, the superb fan vaulting is shown to great effect. Starting from the west door on a left-handed tour, you cannot fail to notice the tomb of Bishop Montague. It is the largest and most lavish as a tribute to his work for the Abbey.

He lies in what looks like an uncurtained four-poster with black columns for bedposts over which heavy high-flown decorations are dangerously balanced above the sleeper. Unusually for a bishop, he is wearing the robes of the Order of the Garter. His brother presented the west door.

On the corner of the north transept stands the black oak figure of King David, from an old organ, playing his harp. Further along on the right you can see through a grating one of the bases of the Norman cathedral.

First English King
Ahead is the Edgar window. Above a Viking ship, the first King of All England is shown receiving the crown from Dunstan, Archbishop of Canterbury, with Oswald, Archbishop of York, standing by. The basis of this service is still used today at a Sovereign's coronation. It is not apparent why Bath was chosen for this ceremony. Perhaps there were political or public relations reasons. Odd too that fourteen years elapsed between Edgar's accession and his crowning in 973.

Falstaff and the Dories
The Abbey is crammed with wall tablets — about 600 altogether. Next to the window, one of them commemorates the colourful witty Georgian actor James Quin. He excelled as Shakespeare's Falstaff and, from an over-indulgent style of living, grew as swollen. His epicurean tastes included a great partiality to John Dories, the sea-water fish.

On three occasions he killed a man in sword-fights but each time escaped virtually without punishment. An epitaph, less respectful than Garrick's lines in the Abbey, went:
"Alas, poor Quin, thy jests and stories
Are quite extinguished, and what more is
There's no John Falstaff, no John Dories."

A Giant Jig-saw Puzzle

The immense east window, depicting scenes from Our Lord's life, was blown out by a land mine during the Second World War. What a painstaking labour it must have been to fit together again 817 square feet of glass: this was achieved when peace returned. Coming back down the south side, Prior William Birde's richly decorated chantry shows his rebus among the elaborate carving. As Prior, he did much to help Bishop King's building programme.

Picnicking

In the south transept you will find the alabaster tomb of Lady Waller. She was the wife of the general commanding the Roundheads against the Royalists at the drawn Battle of Lansdown, just north of the city. The reclining family looks as if it was on a picnic and had finished off a hamper of delicacies from Fortnum and Mason.

The Gallant Six Hundred

Round the corner, back in the nave, and up on the wall is a humble but strangely moving little tablet to Major Thomas Everard Hulton of the 4th Queen's Own Light Dragoons. He was one of the gallant Six Hundred who survived the charge of the Light Brigade at the Battle of Balaclava during the Crimean War. In the former cloisters are some unusual 17th century alms boxes on wooden pillars intended to stand against the wall.

Now a bizarre tailpiece — several thousand people are said to lie buried beneath your feet in the Abbey and three miles of heating pipes keep them warm.

THE PUMP ROOM

In the Palm Court

The few steps from the Abbey to the Pump Room bring you to Bath's second Golden Age, covering most of the 18th century. From a medieval town of three thousand, confined within its Saxon walls, it became a lovely Georgian city of thirty thousand inhabitants. Chaucer's buxom Wife of Bath, with her five successive husbands and more skilled than the Flemish weavers, gave way to the elegant actress Sarah Siddons.

The handsome Pump Room dates from the 1790's when it replaced a smaller one built a hundred years earlier. High on the dignified classical facade an inscription in Greek austerely advises that "Water is best." Inside, during the season, it is packed with visitors refreshing themselves at tables while the Pump Room Trio plays in truly Palm Court style.

"Muddy Moll"

From a bay-window containing a drinking fountain you can look out over the King's Bath. People of distinction had been coming here long before the city's second flourishing. One of them was James I's consort, Anne of Denmark, or "Muddy Moll" as the citizens called her, who came to be cured of her dropsy. Instead, she got a nasty shock when the water seemed to explode in flame just as she was getting in. This upset her so much that she went elsewhere to what became known as the Queen's Bath (demolished late last century).

Bathing Hazards

It was on the whole a rough and squalid business — quite an ordeal for the bathers. The King's Bath was only cleaned out twice a week. Rain and wind had to be endured without protection.

Though mixed bathing in the nude was now forbidden, the wet linen costumes clung too closely to the body. The place stank of sulphur. People smoked while bathing. Layabouts threw each other in. Dogs, cats and pigs were hurled often over the walls into the water.

The King of Bath

In the Pump Room, above a priceless Tompion long-case clock and two Sedan chairs, stands a statue of the man who cleaned all this up and made Bath a well-run fashionable spa. He is dressed in a full-skirted Georgian coat. His portrait in the adjoining sun-lounge shows a flabby face with sensual mouth and double chin. This is of course Richard "Beau" Nash (1674-1761). The nickname came not from his looks but from his extravagant style.

The son of a Swansea bottle manufacturer, he went to Jesus College, Oxford but preferred making love to studying. Then he tried the Army, which paid him too little and expected him to go soldiering in addition to wearing a fancy uniform. After a spell learning the Law, he had his first success as an impresario. This was a pageant, which so pleased William III that a knighthood was offered. Nash declined because no cash went with it.

Wild Oats

When hard-up, he made money by betting on his own misbehaviour. He won £50 for standing outside York Minster wearing only a blanket. On another occasion he rode stark naked through a village on a cow. Then there was the time when he visited some

14

friends on a warship. Roused from a drunken slumber, he found himself sailing off to the Mediterranean. Here the ship saw action in which he was wounded in the leg. This brought no money but later he frequently dined out on the story.

His passion for gambling brought him in 1705 to Bath, where he made a great impression on Captain Webster, the Master of Ceremonies, who made him his gentleman-in-waiting. When the captain was killed in a duel, Nash got the job. Queen Anne's recent visits had attracted many other visitors but the facilities for their safety and entertainment badly needed reorganisation. The new Master of Ceremonies was quickly at work.

Strict Impresario

Balls were to finish promptly at 11 p.m. The carrying of swords was banned. Dress regulations were tightened up. If he met a man wearing boots in a public room, Nash would tell him he had forgotten his horse. Seeing the Marchioness of Queensberry wearing a white apron at a ball, he tore it off and flung it to her maid.

Another time, a gentleman carried away by his wife's "increase of beauty" after treatment in the King's Bath began to pay her "familiar compliments." Nash immediately threw him into the water. In the ensuing duel Nash was wounded in the arm. Eventually he put up everywhere a list of eleven rules of behaviour, which ranged from dress to scandal-mongering.

He was buried with great pomp. The coffin, borne by six aldermen, was followed by "the lame, the emaciated and the feeble." Even the housetops were packed with spectators mourning the loss of their "King".

The Daily Routine

A visitor's day started early with a dip in the baths. Here the ladies would be given a little floating wooden dish, which they tied to their waists. On it might be a handkerchief, a nosegay, a snuffbox and some beauty spots. These patches were sometimes stuck on in certain positions to indicate the time and place of an intended assignation. But in the steamy conditions they often slipped, which led to embarrassing situations.

Next came the first trip to the Pump Room for gossip and drinking the waters. Three pints were usually taken in contrast to the earlier heavy intake of ten. Charles Dickens' Mr. Pickwick went there much later with his devoted servant Sam Weller, who found the water had "a wery strong flavour o' warm flat-irons." A public breakfast was followed by a service in the Abbey. In the afternoon a second visit was made to the Pump Room and the day ended with a play or a public ball.

THE CITY — EAST

Benevolent Tycoon

A Cornish postmistress's grandson named Ralph Allen (1693-1764) was one of the three founders of the city's second great period, together with Nash and the architect John Wood. Allen's chance came when, as a Bath postal official, he reported a wagon-load of illegal arms to General Wade during the first Jacobite rising. In return Wade helped him get a contract to run the country's provincial post. He sorted out this corrupt and inefficient service, making a fortune for himself at the same time.

He made another fortune out of selling Bath stone from his quarries on Combe Down, south of the city. This enabled him to encourage the ambitious building plans for Bath of John Wood, who designed for his patron a magnificent mansion, Prior Park. Located near the quarries, it was frequently used by visiting royalty in Allen's time and is now a public school.

Palladian Splendour

To get to Allen's town house go a little way south from the Abbey and turn left into York Street. On the right a small entrance with an iron gateway leads to a courtyard and the house where he ran his postal business. Now completely blocked in, this shapely residence was built in the Palladian style derived from the 16th century Italian, Andrea Palladio, who revived the splendours of classical Roman architecture.

Back in York Street turn left into Church Street and Abbey Green, a charming little backwater where the monks used to play bowls. A relic of the former monastic precinct, it has an excellent specimen of the town-loving plane tree.

"The Gay Sally Lunn"

Leaving the Green by North Parade Passage (sadly changed from Old Lilliput Alley) you come to Sally Lunn's tea-shop, one of the city's oldest houses. An owl lives behind the gable of this fairy-tale Tudor building. Here is baked the delicacy which so delighted W.S. Gilbert, Sullivan's other half:

"Now for the tea of our host,
Now for the rollicking bun,
Now for the muffin and toast —
Now for the gay Sally Lunn."

However the name of its creator, supposedly a persecuted Huguenot fugitive from France, is open to question. The French have always known her kind of bun as a "Sol et Lune", because it was gold on top and white underneath.

The museum in the cellars is well worth a visit. Seven floors have been excavated to reveal levels from Roman, Saxon and medieval times. You can wonder at stalactites and stalagmites, and early faggot oven, a Georgian cooking-range and a secret cupboard where Sally Lunn's recipe was discovered. There is a fine collection of clay pipes, tracing their history, and also oddments like a Georgian toothbrush and some meat tags of the same period.

Trail-blazer

On the opposite side of the Passage lived John Palmer (1742-1818), the mail-coach pioneer (not to be confused with the prominent contemporary architect of the same name). He began by running fast coaches between his two theatres in Bath and Bristol, enabling the cast and their costumes to appear at both in the same piece on alternate nights.

This was the origin of his scheme for a national mail-coach system. Previously letters had been carried by post-boys on horses. Despite Allen's improvements, it was a painfully slow business and so unreliable that people despatching bank-notes cut them in two and sent the halves separately. Stage-coaches then took thirty-eight hours for the journey between Bath and London but Palmer's "specials" cut that time to under sixteen hours. They were exempt from tolls and toll-gate keepers who did not heed the warning horn were fined.

Soon London was linked with sixteen other towns. Sadly, after a fearful row with Lord Walsingham, the Postmaster-General, Palmer was sacked but went on to become Bath's mayor and MP.

Horatio Home

Continuing along North Parade turn right into Pierrepont Street. On the left at No. 2, Lord Nelson's clergyman father and family came for winter stays to get away from cold, bleak Norfolk. Horatio himself would come too after a spell abroad as a junior naval officer. Next door lived the snooty Georgian statesman, Lord Chesterfield, best known for the boring letters on behaviour he wrote to his natural son. He disliked Bath and also Beau Nash, whom he called "a gilded garland."

A Great Scandal

On the opposite side, through St. James's Portico, is Pierrepont Place. At No. I, behind the heavy Ionic doorway with carved pineapples above, resided the musical Linley family. Their daughter Elizabeth was a dazzling beauty with a fine voice. She caused one of the city's major scandals by eloping at the age of eighteen with the dramatist Richard Brinsley Sheridan.

One of the Linley servants was Emma Hart before she became Lady Hamilton and Nelson's mistress. The building is now a gallery of contemporary art called Artsite.

Titled Bigamy

Turn left into South Parade where No. 5 was briefly the home of the Duchess of Kingston, the notorious 18th century bigamist. When a girl, as Miss Elizabeth Chudleigh, she became a maid of honour to the Princess of Wales. At court her charm and beauty attracted Lord Hervey's naval son, the future Earl of Bristol. They were married but after one disastrous night together he sailed off to the West Indies. Later she had a child which soon conveniently died.

Back at court, where nobody knew of the Hervey affair, she took the fancy of Evelyn Pierrepont, Duke of Kingston, who asked her to marry him. Eventually she and Hervey fiddled an official declaration that their wedding was null and void because it had not been consummated. So she became the Duchess of Kingston. When the Duke died, his nephew — who had been disinherited and had discovered her guilty secret — brought a charge of bigamy against her.

The trial was held with great ceremony before the House of Lords in 1776: it was the fashionable sensation of the year. She was found guilty but her title exempted her from the punishment of being branded on the hand. Soon after she fled to the Continent and died in Paris twelve years later.

Novelists on Parade

Two 18th century novelists lived next door on

South Parade, Sir Walter Scott at No. 6 (as a child) and the less well-known Tobias Smollett at No. 7. Smollett's writing provides lively and highly critical descriptions of Bath's social life. "Here we have nothing but noise, tumult, and hurry." The Pump Room was compared to a Welsh fair with people of "the highest quality, and the lowest trades jostling each other, without ceremony." The city was "a stew pan of idleness and insignificance."

Yet another novelist, Fanny Burney, stayed at No. 14 with Mrs. Thrale, Dr. Samuel Johnson's friend. She gave a vivid account of the anti-Catholic riot in 1780, when hundreds of troops were sent for to disperse the looting, burning mob. The nearby church of St. John was designed by Charles Hansom, brother of the inventor of the famous cab.

The Grotto's Secret
Duke Street leads to North Parade where a short diversion to the right brings you to Delia's Grotto down below the bridge. In this strange little stone hut Sheridan and Elizabeth Linley left their love- letters to each other. From the far end of the bridge, looking south to the heights of Combe Down, you can just make out the columns of Prior Park, Ralph Allen's superb mansion.

Back over the bridge along North Parade, No. II housed two 18th century Irishmen — the author Oliver Goldsmith and later Edmund Burke, the great Whig parliamentary orator. William Wordsworth the poet stayed at No. 9 in 1831.

Sham Folly
Cross to the balustrade of the Grand Parade above Parade Gardens. Here a plaque commemo-

rates the site of the original Assembly Rooms of Thomas Harrison, finished off by declining popularity and a fire. Looking east to Bathampton Down you can discern Sham Castle among the trees. There is nothing behind the front with its gateway and two end towers. Apparently Ralph Allen wanted something to look at from his town house and follies were fashionable in the 18th century. It also gave work at a time of acute unemployment.

The Headless Prince

The Grand Parade opens into Orange Grove with its obelisk, so named after a visit from the Prince of Orange in 1734. He was a stunted hunchback. According to the memoir-writer Lord Hervey, he appeared from behind to have no head and from the front no neck or legs. His breath was most offensive. However, benefiting from the waters, he presented a gold snuffbox to Nash, who thanked him by putting up the obelisk.

Naval Blockade

In front looms the massive imitation Jacobean Empire Hotel, opened in 1901. This is surmounted by what look to be two cottages, a mansion and a castle, all in miniature. The Admiralty took it over at the beginning of the Second World War in 1939 and has not yet moved out.

Behind the hotel in Boat Stall Lane you find the remains of the city's old East Gate — small and unimpressive. The other grander gates were pulled down during the 18th century, although they survive today as street names.

Almost next door, take a glance at the flourishing little market always thronged with hopeful bargain-seekers. Round the corner of Bridge Street the Victoria Art Gallery has a fine dome and an overblown statue of the Queen. Above it the figures of Britannia and India sit glaring at each other.

Ponte Pulteney

Turn right to Pulteney Bridge, one of Bath's showpieces based on the Ponte Vecchio in Florence. It was built to link the city with the estate of the wealthy property owner, Sir William Pulteney, who launched Elizabeth Chudleigh. Crossing the Bridge, you pass on the right-hand side at each end a domed toll-house, joined by a row of small shops with a central Venetian window.

In Argyle Street, on the same side, at No. 9 a pub called "The Boater" has an intriguing bow-windowed Georgian front. Above the shop next door is shown the colourful coat of arms of Queen Charlotte, wife of George III: it was restored after rescue from a Milsom Street basement.

No Column for Nelson

Argyle Street runs into Laura Place, named after Pulteney's daughter. Opposite is a Victorian pillar-box, dating from 1866 and known as a Penfold hexagonal from its designer. The fountain in the middle was put up eleven years later to mark the Bath and West Agricultural Society's centenary. A plan to provide a Nelson's column here in 1805 failed through lack of funds.

In the same year William Pitt (The Younger), Prime Minister at twenty-four, was living at No. 15 Johnstone Street on the corner of Laura Place. Here he received the grim news of Napoleon's victory over the Russians and Austrians at Austerlitz. It shattered his hopes and he died broken-hearted the next year.

Bluestocking and Dyed Hair

Before you stretches Great Pulteney Street — Bath's most impressive, longest (1000 feet) and widest (100 feet). The tour follows the right-hand side of the street. At No. 76 lived Hannah More, the Georgian do-gooder and bluestocking. This term originated in the pretentious literary parties where people wore blue worsted instead of black silk stockings. She wrote a popular novel with the strange title of "Coelebs in Search of a Wife."

Exactly opposite, Lord Lytton, best known as author of "The Last Days of Pompeii", used to stay from 1867 to 1872. By this time although old and deaf, he was described as "the dapper gentleman, with dyed hair and whiskers . . . scrupulously honest in his dealings . . . the reverse of his wife who, thirty years before, had made Bath her home and tradesmen her victims." A little further along on the same side, Thomas Baldwin, the man who designed the street, lived at No. 6 in 1793 before he went bankrupt.

Kicked Upstairs

Outside Nos. 74 and 72 some curious lampholders, known as "throwovers", survive from the 18th century. Louis XVIII stayed at the latter in 1813, the year before being put on the French throne after Napoleon's abdication. High over No. 59 you cannot miss the huge Pulteney coat of arms. Lord Hervey said that Sir William was made Earl of Bath to stop his political meddling in the House of Commons. Opposite is Sunderland Street — about 75 feet long and Bath's shortest.

Shy Songster

Turning right at another Victorian pillar-box into Edward Street, you pass No. 6 where Emma Hart (now Lady Hamilton) stayed in 1809. Nelson had generously bequeathed her to the nation before he died. At No. 10 the small-paned "Gothic" window was installed to stop passers-by peering in at the occupant from 1919 to 1928, Frederick Wetherby. He was a song writer who provided the words for "Danny Boy", "Roses of Picardy", "Up from Somerset" and "The Holy City."

"Strata" Smith

Back in Great Pulteney Street, on the opposite side at No. 29 William Smith in 1799 dictated "The Order of the Strata" to the Rev. Benjamin Richardson. This great work earned him the title of "The Father of English Geology." A short way on, William Wilberforce, the philanthropist largely responsible for the abolition of slavery, lived at No. 36.

Sailor's Quiverful

At the end of Great Pulteney Street, turn right into Sydney Street (New) where on the corner at No. 103 the Duke of Clarence stayed in 1817. A good-natured breezy sailor, he had ten illegitimate children by the actress Mrs. Jordan before becoming King William IV.

Fun in the Shrubbery

The dignified porticoed building which seals off Great Pulteney Street was completed in 1796 as public rooms for Sydney Gardens nearby. It is now the Holburne Museum, housing an array of fine porcelain, paintings and silver. In front you will see two shapely watchman's huts. The Gardens were very popular in their time. Great galas were held there with fireworks and music, while lots of other things went on in the grottoes, labyrinth and bushes.

Shoplifting

Cross over to Sydney Place (Old) where Jane Austen lived at No. 4. Her novels "Persuasion" and "Northanger Abbey" feature Bath frequently but she never liked the place. One reason might have been that her aunt Mrs. Leigh Perrot had been accused of stealing lace from a Bath Street shop on faked evidence. She was found not guilty at her trial, which was packed out.

Jail-birds' Home

Turn right into Sutton Street and walk straight through the quiet seclusion of Henrietta Park, named after the same Pulteney daughter as in Laura Place. Across from the exit, a few steps to the right, a passageway takes you to Grove Street. On the left stands the former New Prison (1772), which looks more domestic than penal. Appropriately it is now a block of flats.

On the right over a window of No. 22, once a coaching station and now refurbished, are the puzzling numbers 5792. This is a Masonic date: the Freemasons' calendar begins in 4000 BC which puts the original building at AD 1792.

The Ducking-stool

Fork right towards the river where on the opposite side below Pulteney Bridge, in bygone days, stood the ducking-stool. This was used to punish scandal-mongers, scolds and fraudulent tradesmen. Passing under Argyle Street, a pleasant riverside walk ends at the North Parade bridge.

THE CITY — NORTH I

Military MP

General Wade found time in his soldiering career to be MP for Bath where he did much to promote its second flowering. Best known for his road building in Scotland, he made such a mess of handling the second Jacobite rising in 1745 that he had to be replaced by the Duke of Cumberland, butcher of Culloden. A bachelor with four illegitimate children, he was uncle to Captain Wade, Nash's third successor as Master of Ceremonies.

Leaving Abbey Churchyard by Wade's Passage, for which he was responsible, his handsome house (now a National Trust shop) is on the left. The Rebecca Fountain you pass was put up in 1861 by the Bath Temperance Association. The enormous number of pubs and taverns in Victorian Bath was rivalled only by the number of people trying to shut them down.

Chandeliered Elegance

On the High Street's right is the neo-classical Guildhall — the city's most majestic public building. The centre was the work of Thomas Baldwin, but the two wings with cupola turrets are late Victorian: should the high-up statue of Justice not be blindfold?

Don't miss the exquisite Banqueting Room, Bath's finest Georgian interior. There is a musicians' gallery and portraits of celebrities adorn the walls between Corinthian half-columns. Among these are Ralph Allen and Wade, who ended up as a field-marshal. The glorious four-tier chandeliers once blazed down on the assembled cream of society.

"Gardyloo!"

Opposite the Guildhall, have a look up The Corridor, an enchanting glass-covered shopping alley, bridged by two musicians' galleries with forlorn statues, garlands and minute lions' heads. Turn left a few yards on into Northumberland Place. Behind its narrow entrance is a charming little street, glowing with flowers in summer and secluded from the bustle all round.

It is crossed by Union Passage — the medieval Lock's Lane, known more vulgarly as Cock Lane. In former times it would have echoed with cries of "Gardyloo!" as slops were flung from windows.

The Good Samaritan

Turn right into Union Street and where it joins Upper Borough this notice is inscribed on the wall: "Royal National Hospital for Rheumatic Diseases. Royal Mineral Water Hospital. Established by Act of Parliament as the Hospital or Infirmary in the City of Bath AD 1739." To your left in Upper Borough Walls over the main entrance is displayed a Victorian carving of The Good Samaritan in action.

This might have been more appropriate for later patients but early on citizens were barred. The impoverished visitors who were admitted had to bring a certificate of recommendation from their parish and also £3. This was to pay either for their burial or their return if cured. Originally known as the General Hospital, it got off to a bad start with the sacking of a surgeon for making indecent examinations of two prostitutes.

Not Before Time

Across the street you can see a Victorian reproduction of the medieval city wall. Behind and below is a courtyard, where a plaque records: "This area of ground was in the year 1736 set apart for the burial of patients dying in the Bath General Hospital and after receiving 238 bodies was closed by the Governors of the Charity in the year 1849 from regard to the health of the living."

The Chinless Wonder

Turn right into Trim Bridge. On the corner house appear the letters SPPP and SMP, which once indicated the parish boundary separating St. Peter and St. Paul's from St. Michael's.

Trim Street, named after the landowner George Trim a wealthy clothier, was one of the first streets to be built in the 18th century outside the city walls. No. 5 was the home of the parents of James Wolfe, the chinless, undersized and ailing general. From here in 1759 he left for Quebec to die victorious in the battle against the French which secured Lower Canada for his country.

"Be Quiet, John Wood"

Pass under St. John's Gate into Queen Street. At Bath City Council meetings, the architect John Wood was always being told to keep quiet. On one occasion when names for new streets were called for, somebody suggested using the words most frequently heard at these meetings. That is the unlikely origin of the names of the three streets which meet where you now stand — Quiet, John and Wood.

In Quiet Street on the right, No. 9 (now housing the Royal Bank of Scotland) was once known as "The Auction Mart and Bazaar." It dates from 1824 and on either side of the fine arched window appear the niched figures of "Commerce" and "Genius." Cross Milsom Street to Green Street, named after a former bowling green nearby. On the left at No. 3 survives an old three-gabled farmhouse with a shell-head doorway. There used to be sheep-pens at the back.

Taking the Biscuit

The famous Bath Oliver was originally baked in Green Street. This plain digestive biscuit had no miraculous curing powers: it was just made from simple ingredients which gave your inside a rest from rich food. Dr. William Oliver, its creator and the General Hospital's first physician, has a restaurant named after him at the end of the street.

Pickwickian Origins

Turn left into Broad Street, where on the right the Saracen's Head flourishes. Although the name conjures up visions of the Crusaders, the inn was built only in 1713. Charles Dickens, when a newspaper reporter, was a lodger in 1835 and here he probably thought up his "Pickwick Papers." The name came either from a village on the London road or from a Bath coach owner called Moses Pickwick.

Double First

Opposite is the Bath Postal Museum. History was made here on 2nd May 1840 with the first known posting of the world's first stamp — the Penny Black. In the window is a behind-the-scenes reconstruction of

31

a 19th century post office, where two employees are taking things very seriously. Dealing with a saucer of milk is the cat, which was on the pay-roll for anti-vermin duties. Quill pens are among the primitive office equipment.

Two Leading Ladies

At the end of Broad Street fork right to the raised pavement of the Vineyards. Some distance along on the left brings the "Gothick" chapel built in 1765 for Selina, Countess of Huntingdon, a fanatical Methodist. Nash severed connections with her when it was rumoured that, after conversion, he was to preach at the Assembly Rooms as the Reverend Richard Nash. This undistinguished battlemented building is now the Huntingdon Centre for the study of Bath's history and architecture.

Across the street towards the end of the Paragon at No. 33 resided a very different sort of lady — Sarah Siddons, the magnetic Georgian actress. The daughter of strolling players from the West Country, she got her first acting chance at Bath. After a shaky start she eventually became such an attraction that the theatres at Bath and Bristol were filled only on the nights of her performance. She even played Hamlet. Thereafter at Drury Lane she was London's most celebrated tragic actress.

Admiral from Down Under

On the left a stiff climb up Guinea Lane brings you to Lansdown Road. Turn left and then right into Bennett Street. Admiral Arthur Phillip retired to No. 19, where he died in 1814. Indeed many naval officers ended their days in Bath, where it was cheaper to live than in London. He had been the founder of Australia. Here he had landed six ship-loads of the first convicts sentenced to transportation and set up a penal settlement at Sydney. The Australian flag flies over his memorial tablet in the Abbey.

From Revels to Bombs

At the end of Bennett Street on the left are the Assembly Rooms. The building was completed in 1771 to cater for the fashionable who had moved from the city's centre to the heights of Lansdown. The plain exterior conceals splendid rooms inside. Here performed such celebrities as Franz Liszt, Johann Strauss and Adelina Patti: Charles Dickens gave readings.

In the 1930's the place was used as a cinema, a billiards saloon and sale-rooms. Carefully restored after suffering severe damage in the Second World War's air raids, the Assembly Rooms now belong to the National Trust.

On with the Dance

The interior had a lavish chandeliered ballroom with seven marble chimney-pieces. The atmosphere must have been overpowering when the fires were roaring and the dancers sweating their guts out. The ballroom was linked by an octagonal card room to the tea-room, equally rich in decoration.

For the minuet hooped skirts were worn but they were banned for the more spirited country dances. Ladies who discarded them would "be assisted by proper servants in an appartment for that purpose." Gentlemen performing the minuet had to wear "a full-trimmed suit of clothes, or French frock, hair or wig dressed in a bag."

These rules were strictly enforced by the Master of Ceremonies Captain Wade. He had been appointed after a riot among the contenders for the job but later blotted his copy-book by seducing the wife of a prominent citizen and had to resign.

Fashions and Hairstyles

In the basement is the Museum of Custume, one of the finest collections in the world. On entering you are greeted by the bust of an admiral with a most unusual name — Sir Cloudesley Shovel. He is best known for losing two thousand lives in four ships wrecked off the Scillies in 1707.

You can admire a fascinating variety of costumes, beautifully displayed. The exhibits range from a linen baby's bonnet, showing the date of 18th April 1733 to the toque Queen Mary wore at the 1935 Jubilee celebrations.

Perhaps the most curious item is an 18th century procelain wig-scraper. At that time mens' wigs were dressed with an ointment called pomatum or simply with tallow fat or hog's grease. After being powdered and curled with heated clay rollers, they were sometimes baked.

Women did not usually wear wigs. Their own long hair was often made up into styles of exaggerated height and width with pads of horse-hair and wool. However the "ship in full sail" style is mythical. So too are suggestions of mouse-traps being inserted to catch the mice supposed to be living in the hair. Reports of head lice and unpleasant smells should not be taken too seriously.

34

THE CITY — NORTH 2

Eagles on the Ceiling

Leave Abbey Churchyard by the Colonnade with its unfluted Ionic pillars and turn right into Stall Street. This was named after the now vanished church of St. Mary de Stalls, probably derived from Mary of the Manger. The five bollards on the corner of Cheap Street were put there to prevent heavy vehicles from collapsing into the cellars below.

Turn left into Westgate Street where an upstairs room at the Grapes Hotel has a most unusual ceiling. It is Jacobean and probably Bath's earliest surviving plaster-work. The ornate design consists of three main centre pieces in which a double-headed eagle and a leopard's head between two Tudor roses are spaced alternately. There are many other emblems, masks and figures as well.

These escutcheons may have belonged to Charles Granville, second Earl of Bath. For fighting against the Turks in 1683 he was created a Count of the Holy Roman Empire, which entitled him to the Roman Eagle in his coat of arms.

The Third Founder

Cross over into Monmouth Street and turn right up Princes Street which leads to Queen Square, named after Caroline, George II's consort. This is surely the finest achievement here of John Wood the architect and third of the founders of Georgian Bath.

Almost certainly born in the city, he had ambitious plans for making it a second Rome but they were never fully realised. However, under the patronage of Ralph Allen, he was responsible for a great building expansion in the Palladian style. With little proper education, he seems to have been a strange and rather unpleasant person.

"Poor Fred"

The obelisk in the middle of the Square was erected by Nash in honour of the visiting Frederick, Prince of Wales. He was loathed by his parents, George II and Queen Caroline. She said of him: "My dear first-born is the greatest ass and the greatest liar and the greatest 'canaille' and the greatest beast in the whole world, and I heartily wish he were out of it." "Poor Fred", who never succeeded to the throne, added to Nash's collection of snuffboxes, which accounts for the obelisk.

A Handsome Palace

As you enter the Square, the corner house on the right, No. 13, was where Jane Austen wrote much of her novel "Northanger Abbey." Straight ahead at the end of the west side is Bath's most important piece of architecture, according to the experts. Here the whole range of the north side looks like a handsome palace with its Corinthian half-columns and central urn-topped pediment.

Linkboys and Wigs

Passing in front of it you will notice the ornamental lampholders above the basement steps of No. 21 and the 18th century lamplighters' snuffer over the doorway of No. 22-23. These snuffers were used for putting out the flaming torches of the linkboys who lit the way for the sedan chairs. John Wood is recorded as having lived at No. 24 but his house was probably No. 9 on the south side, from which he could admire his masterpiece.

Turn left into Gay Street and on the opposite side bow-cornered No. 41 was the home of John Wood's son — another John. You will see through a ground-floor window a curious little circular tile-covered room where Georgian gentry powdered and fitted their wigs. Up on the left-hand side No. 8 was specially designed for Robert Gay, a London surgeon. He owned the land now occupied by Queen Square and Gay Street.

Dr. Johnson Snubbed

It was also the residence of Mrs. Hester Piozzi. She had been Mrs. Thrale, the dearest friend of Dr. Samuel Johnson. When her husband died, she married an Italian musician called Gabriele Piozzi instead of the doctor as expected. He was so put out that he would have nothing more to do with her and burnt her letters — but she published his. In 1821 on her eightieth birthday, she gave a magnificent ball at the Assembly Rooms, where she danced "with astonishing elasticity" till early next morning. She died the same year — perhaps the ball had been a mistake.

Bath's Colosseum

Gay Street runs straight into the Circus, designed by John Wood. He died soon after starting the work which was completed by his son. The three entrances are equally spaced and whichever way you come in, you are faced with buildings. This gives a feeling of containment at once.

The Circus is based on Rome's Colosseum. Three different orders of classical architecture are shown on the front of each house: the ground-floor columns are Doric (plain), the first floor Ionic (rams' heads) and the second floor Corinthian (acanthus leaves).

Bladud's Acorns

Just above the doorways an uncommon frieze runs all the way round. It shows symbols of the arts and sciences: there are over five hundred, most of them different subjects — heraldry, weapons, masonic signs, mathematical instruments, tragic masks, flowers, fruit and foliage. In memory of King Bladud, the parapet at the top is adorned with stone acorns, the food of his herd of swine.

The Gouty Commoner

Turn left into the Circus where at Nos. 7 and 8, the only house with two doors, lived William Pitt, Earl of Chatham and known as "The Great Commoner." Unlike his son, Pitt and Younger (already mentioned in the first walk-about), he never became Prime Minister but masterminded the defeat of the French in India and Canada. He is perhaps better known for his chronic gout and it is ironic that he should have been the MP for Bath of the healing waters. His warmongering brought about a quarrel with Ralph Allen, who had been a close friend. However, they became reconciled and Allen left him £1000 in his will.

Empire Builders

Back in England in 1864 after discovering the Zambesi River, the great explorer David Livingstone stayed briefly in the basement of No. 13. Next door lived Lord Clive, the conqueror of India, just before his suicide in 1774. This was caused by the jealousy of his many enemies.

The splendid group of plane trees in the middle was not always there. Originally the area had been a covered reservoir, where servants collected water for the houses which had no pipes. It was paved all over with cobble-stones.

Painter and Spy

In 1759 Thomas Gainsborough lived at No. 17. He had been discovered by the eccentric Philip Thicknesse, who brought him to Bath, where he became famous for his portraits of celebrities. Here he also took up music, his other great interest, but could not apply himself to mastering the notes. After a stupid row with Thicknesse, he moved to London and even greater success.

No. 22 housed Major André, a cloak-and-dagger soldier. During the War of American Independence, he was caught by the Americans negotiating with their traitor Benedict Arnold and executed as a spy in 1789.

Photos and Stamps

Leave the Circus by Gay Street. On the left-hand side at No. 23 the late-Victorian pioneer photographer William Friese-Greene set up his studio before moving to the Corridor. Sadly, this charming and talented man died in penury but he got a great funeral.

Turn left to the raised pavement of George Street, once the shopping centre for the upper classes of the Circus and the Royal Crescent. It was one of the first streets to be paved with wooden blocks which reduced the noice of the horse-traffic.

A little way along, at No. 13, this notice appears: "These premises were formerly occupied by the philatelist Henry Stafford Smith (B. 1843 D. 1903), who with his brother Alfred William Smith (B. 1837 D. 1880) published from 1863 onwards 'The Stamp Collector's Magazine.' This was the pioneer philatelic journal and Bath is therefore the cradle city of philatelic literature."

A Multipurpose Building

Turn right into Milsom Street and on the left-hand side the front of No. 43 announces: "Circulating Library and Reading Room." Below is: "State Lottery Office." This was operated from the Library between 1824 and 1830. Here too was the Octagon which began in 1767 as a chapel: the versatile William Herschel, who discovered the planet Uranus in 1781, was its organist. Today it is the headquarters of the Royal Photographic Society, which holds exhibitions there: it also houses a display of the History of Photography.

Two Photographic Pioneers

Continue into Old Bond Street, turning left for New Bond Street. On the opposite side at No. 1 New Bond Street Place two plaques appear on the wall. The first reads: "To perpetuate the name and memory of John Arthur Roebuck Rudge, who lived for many years in the adjoining house and after numerous experiments conducted in the basement was the first Englishman to produce moving pictures by means of photographs mounted on a revolving drum."

The second goes on: "And also to his friend William Friese-Greene who had his studio at No. 9 The Corridor nearby. The inventor of commerical kinematography, being the first man to apply celluloid ribbon for this purpose. Kinematography can thus be attributed to the labours of these two citizens of Bath where this wonderful invention undoubtedly received its birth."

THE CITY — NORTH-WEST
"Bobs"

Starting from the north-west corner of Queen Square, on your left is Queen's Parade, an attractive little terrace. Early this century a frquent visitor to No. 9 was Field Marshal Lord Roberts, who won the Victoria Cross in the Indian Mutiny. For his many campaigns in defence of the Queen's far-flung Empire, he became a hero figure, popularly known as "Bobs". No. 10 was the home of Mrs. Maria Fitzherbert, morganatic wife of the dissolute Prince of Wales, who succeeded as King George IV.

Carrying On

A short diversion of the right along Queen's Parade Place reveals a matching pair of small buildings. They were used as shelters by the sedan chair-men while their passengers visited No. 24 Queen Square and are probably the only ones in England.

These chairs — boxes with poles attached for the carriers — were ideally suited to the city's narrow streets. Invalids could be taken from bed to bath. But they could be very uncomfortable. In wet weather the occupants, still perspiring after the hot mineral waters, were likely to catch a chill from the saturated interiors.

The chair-men had to be strong to cope with Bath's hills. They were a truculent lot and awkward passengers could be either trapped inside or exposed to the elements. Their insolence often provoked gentlemen into drawing their swords and the chair-men would defend themselves with their poles. Eventually Nash imposed some sort of discipline. The hire of a chair was sixpence (2½p) for 500 yards or three shillings (15p) for two miles.

The sedans were replaced in Victorian times by the three-wheeled and pulled Bath chair. These too faded out, only six being left in 1937.

Behind the Facade

Turn back and cross to the steps leading to Gravel Walk beside the Royal Victoria Park's lion-topped entrance gates. The Walk runs along the back of the Gay and Brock Street houses, some of which have unsightly additions. These were necessitated by the early lack of toilet facilities behind the elegant facades. Pits were dug in the basements: when full they were emptied by "nightmen." The few outdoor toilets froze up in winter. Ladies announced they were bound for the garden to "pluck a rose" and disappeared among the bushes. So those ugly bulges were the first attempts at indoor sanitation.

Parisian Barbarism

Above an open grassy space lies the graceful Palladian curve of the younger Wood's Royal Crescent. He built No. 1 for his father-in-law, Thomas Brock. Its first distinguished occupant in 1787 was the Princesse de Lamballe, friend of the ill-fated Queen Marie Antoinette. During the French Revolution, the Parisian mob brandished her severed head on a pike in front of the horrified Queen.

Then came the grand old Duke of York, who marched his ten thousand men up and down that hill. Now tastefully restored, decorated and furnished in 18th century style, it is open to the public. The basement has a Kitchen Museum. Behind No. 1 you can see No. 1A, which was a farmhouse built fifty years before the Crescent.

Sniping at the City

Christopher Anstey, who in 1766 wrote "The New Bath Guide", lived at No. 5. These satirical poems about Bath became a bestseller and he ended up in Westminster Abbey's Poets Corner. This sample snipes at Bath's doctors:

"Since the Day that King BLADUD first found
   out the Bogs,
And thought them so good for himself and his
   Hogs,
Not one of the Faculty ever has try'd
These excellent Waters to cure his own Hide."

Elopement and Duels

One evening in 1772 Elizabeth Linley sneaked off from No. 11 in a sedan chair. Her parents were out and this was the first step in her elopement with Richard Sheridan. The family had moved to No. 11 after living in Pierrepont Place (as mentioned in the first walk-about). On the Continent the couple went through some form of marriage ceremony. Back in England, Sheridan fought two duels with a former admirer of Elizabeth. After that there was a proper wedding, which brought about a very happy marriage. His play "The Rivals", set in Bath, is based on such exploits.

Abstemious Workaholic

No. 17 was the residence of Sir Isaac Pitman, who died there in 1897. He came to Bath as an impecunious young teacher and went on to invent the world's most successful shorthand system. But his attempts to reform the spelling of English failed. Pitman was a lifelong teetotaller, vegetarian, non-smoker and anti-vaccinationist. He started work each day at 6.30 a.m.

A journalist who once asked to see his study was told that it was his office. ("I do not study, I work.") He loved Bath, which he thought the most beautiful city in the country.

The Yellow Door

The owner of No. 22 was probably the Crescent's most eccentric resident. This was Miss Amabel Wellesley-Colley, a descendant of the Duke of Wellington. She painted her front door a loud yellow, quite out of keeping with all the others. This upset the City Council which took action against her in the 1970's. She was also ordered to remove the matching blinds and a window guard shaped like a barbecue grille: this she found necessary as a protection when sunbathing for her rheumatism.

A stubborn rejection of all complaints led to a public enquiry ordered by the Minister of the Environment. She won her case on a technicality and repainted the door a bright primrose. Later she was summonsed for riding a bicycle in Hyde Park's Rotten Row. Conditionally discharged, she "cycled off wearing . . . a luminous orange golf cap." Today the grille has gone and the door is a faded primrose colour.

A Gory Murder

The low wall which runs between the Crescent's two ends was part of what is known as a "ha-ha." This gave the residents a view unspoilt by fence or hedge: it also prevented the cattle which once grazed lower down from using the grass immediately in front of the houses.

Turn right along Marlborough Buildings, put up to stop the prevailing westerly winds blowing across the Crescent. This was the scene of a gory murder in 1828. Richard Gilham, an elderly spinster's servant, bludgeoned and cut the throat of her maid Maria, who had said nasty things about him. Blaming some imaginary robbers, he nearly got away with it but rightly finished up on the gallows.

Solid Doric

Continue up Cavendish Road with its five "throwovers". At the top on the left is the robust Doric House, a villa in the Grecian style with massive columns. It was built for the painter Thomas Barker, who came to Bath from Wales in 1782, and provided a picture gallery for him. Cross over to some steps opposite, where a footpath climbs up to Somerset Place. Its chief feature is an open-topped curving pediment with carved drapery and urn — unique in Bath.

Ahead, beyond Lansdown Place West, stretches the elegant sweep of Lansdown Crescent. You will admire along the broad pavement the stylish lampholders, where soft lights once welcomed the carriages home from private parties or the Assembly Rooms.

Super-follyman

No. 20 was the home of the eccentric millionaire misfit William Beckford. A gifted author, collector and builder, he is mainly remembered for the super-folly he created at Fonthill in the wilds of Wiltshire. This was a colossal Gothic Abbey with a tower which fell down three times. Compelled by debt to sell it, he moved to

Bath in 1822.

He first bought No. 20 and then No. 1 Lansdown Place West. The two were separated by a roadway which he bridged. He soon got rid of the latter and bought No. 19 on the other side as a barrier against noise to which he was very sensitive. Behind, he acquired a lot of ground extending a mile to the top of Lansdown Hill. This he elaborately landscaped and at the summit built a tower, which gave him "the finest prospect in Europe." It has not yet fallen down.

Though a recluse by nature, Beckford was sometimes seen in Bath's book-shops and picture galleries, a small man in the dress of a country squire. He had never been accepted by society owing to an unsavoury homosexual scandal in his early years. He died, aged eighty-four, in 1844 and is buried in a pink granite sarcophagus of his own design at the foot of his tower.

"The Nicest Girl in the Room"

Returning from No. 20, turn left opposite Lansdown Place West into All Saints Road. This leads to a narrow footpath winding down through Park Street to St. James's Square. On the bottom left-hand corner at No. 35 around 1846 lived the quarrelsome poet and writer Walter Savage Landor: he was one of the few literary figures who loved Bath. Here, many years earlier, seeing a lady at a ball, he said: "That's the nicest girl in the room and I'll marry her" — which he did. He was very fond of children and in Bath his dog Pomero used to perform tricks for them.

Handel and Margaret

From St. James's Square (via St. James's Street)

cross Julian Road and keep right of the grass triangle into Upper Church Street. At the bottom the house on the corner of Brock Street was once the home of John Christopher Smith (formerly Schmidt). He became secretary to the composer Handel and when the great man's blindness started in 1751, his amanuensis.

In Brock Street take a glance up Margaret's Buildings on the left. This charming little retreat, bright with flowers in tubs and on lamp-posts, is for pedestrians only. The name comes from the site of a nearby chapel called after Mrs. Margaret Garrard, Lady of the Manor. On the opposite side of Brock Street, No. 16's Gothic style porch was obviously designed for somebody of exceptional height. Now you are at the Circus.

THE CITY — WEST

Osric and Edgar

From Abbey Churchyard turn left into Stall Street and right into Bath Street. The colonnades were provided as a covered way to and from the Pump Room. At the end on the left, No. 8 has two statues over the doorway. The left-hand one is the Mercian sub-king Osric, who founded a nunnery in Bath and the other is King Edgar, crowned in the Abbey. They are believed to have come from the High Street's former Town Hall.

The King that Never Was

In front appears the Cross Bath, so called because it once had a cross in the middle. This was replaced by another in honour of a visit in 1687 of King James II's wife, Mary of Modena, to bring about pregnancy. The waters seem to have done their stuff, since she produced a male heir to the throne, who became the "Old Pretender."

Suspicions were aroused that the birth had been a fiddle. But it was all to no avail, for King James and his family soon fled to France after William of Orange had landed at Torbay. The cross has now disappeared but King Bladud still presides on the inside wall.

Hot Stuff

Just below the Cross Bath on the right is a house with a pillared portico. Its front wall shows in faded lettering: "Hetling Pump Room." This was the pump room where Jane Austen's brother Edward came in 1799 for treatment. He lived to be eighty-four so the waters may have done him some good. Opposite on the corner of Beau Street stands the unpretentious Hot Bath (1773) with its Doric columns and pediment. Here the temperature of the spa water was 118 °F (48 °C) — hence the name.

Elizabethan Grandeur

Turn right to Westgate Buildings and you come at once to Abbey Church House on the right. This gabled and mullioned Elizabethan mansion numbered royalty among its distinguished guests. John Wood called it "the second Best House in the City." Later it became the headquarters of the agricultural society now known as the Royal Bath and West. The building was badly damaged in the 1942 air raids but has been carefully restored. It is today the Abbey Parish House.

From Cattle to Chaplin

Westgate Buildings leads into Sawclose, earlier a timber-yard and then a cattle market. Behind the houses on the right was the site of the old cockpit where birds once fought and also bears were baited. On the same side you pass a bingo hall, formerly the Palace Theatre before closing in 1965. Between the two World Wars, Gracie Fields gave one of her first stage performances here. Before that, it had presented the youthful Charlie Chaplin.

Victorian Virtues

Backing the car-park is the Blue Coat School, founded in 1711, but the present building is mid-Victorian. At the re-opening each boy was given an oak box and each girl an oak pincushion made from the timber of the previous structure. It was a charity school for a hundred children who were put out to apprenticeship or employment at the age of fourteen. It closed in 1920 and the place is now local government offices.

Inside is a tablet with an over-effusive tribute to the work, stretching over a half-century, of Mr. and Mrs. Crowder, a Victorian headmaster and his wife: "Firmly attached to the doctrine and principles of the Church of England, they imparted to many successive generations of scholars a religious and useful education, enforced and illustrated by their own Christian characters, unobtrusive piety and conscientious performance of their duties."

Nash at Home

Across Sawclose, the Theatre Royal is flanked by two of Beau Nash's houses. He lived first on the left at what is now the Garrick's Head, which displays a 150-year-old bust of the famous actor over the entrance. It must have been an imposing house once but part of it has been incorporated in the theatre.

Nash had to make a move in the 1740's because his finances had collapsed. So the second house, tucked away in a corner, is far less grand, though its doorway has fine Corinthian columns with carved eagles above.

A Wiltshire Cheese

Probably Nath's most used quote is: "A man can no more be termed a whoremonger for having one whore in his house than a cheesemonger for having one cheese." Actually he had two but not at the same time. Fanny Murray, who departed to London and a respectable marriage, was succeeded by Juliana Popjoy.

When he first found this country girl from Wiltshire, "she rode about the streets of Bath on a dapple-grey horse; in her hand she carried a many-thonged whip, and hence she was known as Lady Betty Besom."

She nursed Nash through the last five years of his life and then returned to Wiltshire. Here she is supposed to have taken up residence for the rest of her days in a large hollow tree, sleeping on "a lock of straw." Today Nash's home is a thriving restaurant. A notice outside says that Juliana's ghost, dressed in grey, is occasionally seen keeping an eye on things.

The Great Fire

Built in 1805, the Theatre Royal attracted the top actors and actresses of the day — Macready, Kean, Sarah Siddons and Mrs. Jordan, mistress of the Duke of Clarence. Then came the great fire of 1862 which gutted the place and the rebuilding produced today's unimpressive entrance.

At the re-opening the following year the cast of "A Midsummer Night's Dream" including a very young Ellen Terry. After that appeared Sir Henry Irving, Sarah Bernhardt, Mrs. Patrick Campbell and Anna Pavlova, who danced "The Dying Swan" in 1920. The stage's new curtains were presented by Sir Charles Chaplin's widow, Oona: two "C's" are embroidered on them in gold.

Theatrical Phantoms

The Grey Lady, who is the theatre's resident ghost, wears a long grey dress and feathers in her hair.

She slams doors and is most often seen in one of the boxes: sometimes there is just the smell of her very strong jasmine scent in the corridors. She seems to have been one of the theatre's first actresses. Either because of unrequited love or the murder of her lover, she hanged herself in the Garrick's Head, which she also haunts.

The theatre has a curious superstition. Whenever a dead butterfly is found, something nasty always follows. But the sight of a live one fluttering around is a good omen and the butterfly has become the theatre's lucky charm.

Too Many Windows

At the top of Sawclose turn left into Beaufort Square. The left-hand side is filled by the majestic facade of the theatre's original entrance, much more suitable than its present front round the corner. George III's coat of arms and a frieze of garlands and tragic masks are displayed. Charming ornamental lampholders span the gates.

Some of the buildings opposite have filled-in windows. This was to avoid paying the tax levied in 1697 on houses which had more than six windows and a rental value over £5 a year. It was repealed in 1851.

One Man Band

Turn into Monmouth Street which on the right leads through Charles Street to New King Street. At No. 9 on the left Richard Sheridan was living when he eloped with Elizabeth Linley. No. 19 was the home of Sir William Herschel: the plaque outside, put up in 1898, is Bath's first. The son of a Hanoverian regimental bandsman, he was sent to England for his health. He came to Bath as organist to Milsom Street's Octagon Chapel and played in the Pump Room band. He also sang tenor and composed music.

George's Star

His hobby, which was astronomy, became an obsession. On one occasion he polished a mirror continuously for sixteen hours. His sister Caroline would have to put food into his mouth to keep him going. They moved into No. 19 where the garden had enough room for his seven-foot telescope and all its equipment.

Here in 1781 came his remarkable discovery, which doubled the size of the known solar system. He called it Georgium Sidus (George's Star) in honour of the King. But the planet's name was changed to Uranus. Soon after, Herschel left Bath to become George III's court astronomer, with a knighthood later.

The house is now a museum. Inside you will find a replica of the telescope he used to discover Uranus. There is also a selection of the many musical instruments he played, together with the remains of the organ pipes and keyboard from the Octagon Chapel.

An Unusual Relic

From New King Street continue along Great Stanhope Street and turn left into Norfolk Crescent, named after Nelson's home county. Nos. 1 to 7 have been successfully restored after being badly knocked about in the 1942 air raids. These killed 417 people and seriously injured 350 more: about 1200 houses were destroyed or severely damaged, while another 19,000 suffered in lesser ways.

The Crescent has a curious feature on the grass opposite No. 1. This is a small stone building which looks like an overgrown pillar-box but is a watchman's hut. In the 18th century before there were any police, householders got together and employed watchmen to guard their homes. Shelters were provided for them, like this little hut which dates from 1793.

With Love from Napoleon

Leave Norfolk Crescent by Nile Street (from Nelson's naval victory) and cross the Upper Bristol Road. Here a footpath through a car-park leads to the Royal Victoria Park. Ahead is a delightfully nostalgic bandstand. In rose beds on either side are two big stone vases under pillared canopies. According to the inscription, Napoleon gave them to his Empress Josephine and the initial "J" can still be seen. They were brought from France after the Peninsular War and in 1874 presented to the Park.

"Will Ye No Come Back Again?"

A left-hand turn along the Royal Avenue brings you through sphinx-topped gates to the gigantic Victoria Obelisk, put up for Princess Victoria's coming of age in 1837. It is guarded by three lions — two alert and one yawning. She made just one visit to Bath in the whole of her life: that was in 1830, when she was only ten and graciously assented to the new park being named after her.

Nobody really knew why she never came back. Some said that she had overheard a remark about the fatness of her ankles when she appeared on her hotel balcony. Others thought that Prince Albert told her that he had been described as a German during a reception at the railway station in 1843. She did pass through Bath in 1899. Though the train slowed down and the spectators observed her standing up, her expression could not be seen.

Affairs of Honour

Return along the Royal Avenue and you are back at the Park's main entrance with its lion gates. Just before reaching them, in a hollow on the right, is the old Duelling Ground. It was a handy spot on the city's outskirts for making a quick get-away if somebody got killed.

Duelling was banned by the man who will always symbolise the city's Golden Age — Richard "Beau" Nash, uncrowned King of Bath.